ELEVATE YOUR PRODUCTIVITY USING CHATGPT

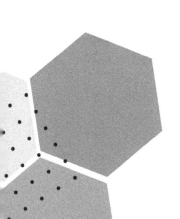

ELEVATE YOUR PRODUCTIVITY USING CHATGPT

An In-Depth Resource for Amplifying Efficiency with Generative AI Technology

Mindscape Artwork Publishing
Mauricio Vasquez
Toronto, Canada

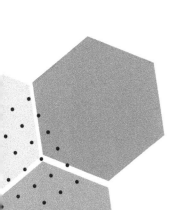

Elevate Your Productivity Using ChatGPT by Mindscape Artwork Publishing [Aria Capri International Inc.]. All Rights Reserved.

Authors:
Mauricio Vasquez

First Printing: November 2023

ISBN - 978-1-998402-31-1 (Paperback)
ISBN - 978-1-998402-30-4 (Hardcover)

SHARE YOUR INSIGHTS

Invest a minute to enhance someone's productivity journey. Your insights can guide professionals in navigating complex work environments and seeking effective productivity strategies.

If "Elevate Your Productivity Using ChatGPT" has helped streamline your tasks or innovate your workflow, please share your experiences in a review. Your feedback can:

- Direct others to effective productivity tools and techniques.
- Help individuals master AI-driven efficiency.
- Transform professional lives through enhanced task management.

Enjoyed the book? Scan the QR code to leave a review where you purchased it. Your review is invaluable and helps foster a community of productivity-focused professionals.

Thank you for contributing to a more efficient and productive world.

Best regards,

Mauricio

Deciphering AI and the Mechanics of ChatGPT

Artificial Intelligence (AI) encompasses the technological advancements aimed at creating computer entities capable of tasks that, until now, distinctly required human cognitive processes. This field incorporates diverse methodologies, including the realms of machine learning and natural language processing (NLP).

ChatGPT represents a specialized segment of AI, employing a subset of machine learning known as deep learning to emulate conversational human text. Its education occurs in a dual-phase approach: initial pretraining followed by targeted fine-tuning.

In the pretraining stage, **ChatGPT absorbs an extensive corpus of text data sourced from the web.** Its primary task is to anticipate subsequent words in a text sequence, using the given context without direct answers—this self-driven learning paradigm hones its linguistic structure, knowledge acquisition, logic, and overall linguistic proficiency.

Subsequently, the model undergoes fine-tuning with a curated dataset, incorporating interactive examples and comparative evaluations. AI trainers contribute by simulating dialogues, acting as both the query source and the AI respondent, further supported by a suite of machine-generated suggestions.

They appraise the varying responses to refine the model's performance and encourage adherence to intended behaviors.

Such rigorous training endows ChatGPT with a nuanced understanding of language context, thus enabling it to generate pertinent and coherent discourse. It assimilates observed data patterns, extrapolating these to deliver effective communication in a multitude of scenarios.

In live interactions, **ChatGPT processes the input text, breaks it down into analyzable components, and crafts replies based on its extensive learned patterns, always striving for relevance and consistency within the conversational thread.** It is a product of vast data-driven learning, aimed at perfecting language interpretation and response accuracy. Nevertheless, it's essential to recognize that ChatGPT, like any model, is susceptible to errors, and users should critically assess its output.

ChatGPT stands as a prominent example of artificial intelligence in contemporary use, but it is far from being the pioneer of AI tools integrated into daily life. Here's a list of AI applications you're likely already familiar with:

1. Virtual Assistant:
Employ ChatGPT in the role of a virtual aide to organize reminders, arrange your schedule, maintain task lists, and field common questions.

2. Personalized Recommendations:
Utilize ChatGPT's ability to curate bespoke suggestions for dining, accommodation, entertainment, reading, or leisure activities that align with your tastes, aiding in more enlightened choices.

3. Language Enhancement:
Interact with ChatGPT to refine and advance your proficiency in foreign languages through active dialogue practice and writing assistance.

4. Quick Fact-Finding:
Pose questions to ChatGPT, request detailed clarifications, or obtain speedy insights on a broad spectrum of subjects, akin to an internet search.

5. Progress Monitoring and Encouragement:
ChatGPT can serve as your accountability partner in monitoring your milestones, supplying encouraging nudges, or proposing strategies to maintain your concentration.

6. Intellectual Discovery:
Leverage ChatGPT as a tool for intellectual pursuits, to probe into specific areas of interest, or to unearth novel insights and data.

Functional Scope and Practical Applications

ChatGPT's mastery of natural language processing allows it to grasp and process conversational input effectively. This characteristic, combined with its user-friendly interface and accessibility, renders it an influential instrument that significantly amplifies productivity and the acquisition of knowledge for its users.

The model's design to preserve conversational context over a dialogue sequence enables it to recall and integrate past interactions into subsequent responses, enhancing the accuracy and relevance of its communication. **ChatGPT is adept at fielding factual questions, elucidating concepts, providing definitions, and facilitating the pursuit of general knowledge.**

ChatGPT's deep understanding of language nuances and its contextual recall feature allows it to produce responses that are not only precise but also appropriately tailored to the conversation at hand. As a result, **ChatGPT stands as a valuable ally for various informational requisites.**

Spanning an array of functions such as customer service, editorial assistance, language acquisition, personal task management, coding support, and intellectual discovery, ChatGPT's versatility is a boon for augmenting efficiency and productivity across diverse domains.

However, **it is essential to acknowledge ChatGPT's limitations**. It might not offer the specialized expertise found in domain-specific professionals or fully supplant human judgment. Caution should be exercised when dealing with context sensitivity and managing sensitive or confidential material while deploying AI tools like ChatGPT, particularly in professional settings.

Despite these caveats, **integrating ChatGPT into workplace practices can yield significant advantages.** It is poised to simplify complex workflows, enhance team collaboration, and provide multifaceted assistance in numerous job-related activities. Organizations that leverage ChatGPT's strengths can cultivate a more streamlined, innovative, and productive work culture.

Optimizing Work with ChatGPT

In the rhythm of today's dynamic professional landscapes, efficiency isn't just a benefit—it's a necessity. ChatGPT emerges as a multifaceted tool, ready to enhance your productivity and streamline your daily tasks. **Embrace these ten actionable methods to fully leverage ChatGPT's capabilities and transform the way you work.** Embark on this innovative path to work more intelligently and achieve greater accomplishments.

ChatGPT stands as an indispensable ally in your professional toolkit, replacing lengthy information hunts with instant, accessible insights. Whether it's a nudge for your next task, a co-author for your communications, or a partner in problem-solving, ChatGPT is equipped to elevate your workday experience. Join in as we discover how ChatGPT can be a game-changer in your workflow. Prepare to tap into heightened productivity and welcome a new epoch of workplace efficiency. Here are a few avenues through which ChatGPT can be utilized in the workplace:

1. Rapid Information Access:
ChatGPT accelerates the retrieval of pertinent information, definitions, or clarifications on work-related subjects, minimizing the time dedicated to locating suitable references.

2. Task Organization:
ChatGPT can be your digital organizer, setting up reminders, overseeing task lists, and keeping your daily schedule on track to ensure that no deadline or appointment slips through the cracks.

3. Editorial Assistance:
Need a second pair of eyes on your written work? ChatGPT can offer editorial guidance, from drafting communiqués to refining reports, ensuring your written communication is polished and precise.

4. Training and Onboarding:
ChatGPT serves as an on-demand training assistant, addressing frequent queries during employee orientation or elucidating company protocols and guidelines.

7. Analytical Reasoning:
Deploy ChatGPT's analytical prowess to brainstorm, evaluate alternatives, and scrutinize data, bolstering more strategic decision-making in your role.

8. Coding and Technical Insights:
For those in technical fields, ChatGPT can dispense coding advice, debug strategies, or demystify intricate technological concepts.

9. Enhancing Customer Interactions:
Embed ChatGPT within customer service frameworks for immediate customer engagement, tackling common inquiries, and potentially trimming down wait times.

10. Creative Collaboration:
Utilize ChatGPT as a sounding board to kindle creativity, uncover fresh viewpoints, or drive group brainstorming initiatives, nurturing innovation and teamwork.

11. Project Oversight:
ChatGPT can aid in monitoring project trajectories, updating progress, and reminding you of upcoming milestones, contributing to proficient project governance.

12. Support for Employee Wellness:
Employ ChatGPT as a resource for employee health and happiness, offering advice on managing stress, balancing work and personal life, or navigating to mental health support channels.

Streamlining Sales and Marketing with ChatGPT

In the swiftly evolving realm of commerce, sales and marketing divisions are on a perpetual quest for cutting-edge strategies to not only attract and assess leads but also cultivate tailored engagements with customers. A formidable ally in this quest is ChatGPT.

1. ChatGPT for Enhancing Lead Dynamics

The traditional methods of lead generation and qualification are often labor-intensive, involving cold calls, email campaigns, and meticulous data scrutiny. ChatGPT introduces a transformative approach by automating and refining these processes.

When integrated into digital platforms, ChatGPT can interact with potential clients via your website or messaging apps, initiating dialogue, posing strategic inquiries, and gathering crucial prospect data. Its adeptness in natural language processing enables it to sift through responses, discerning levels of interest and identifying high-potential leads.

This shift to automation liberates the sales force to channel their expertise towards the most viable prospects, thereby bolstering efficiency and elevating conversion rates.

2. Personalized Customer Interactions Made Effortless

The cornerstone of enduring customer relationships and loyalty lies in personalized interactions. ChatGPT steps in to automate these exchanges without forfeiting the personalized essence. It can autonomously manage chat-based customer support, instantly resolving common questions and engaging in fluid, context-aware conversations that resonate on a personal level with each customer.

By incorporating insights from customer history, like previous purchases and preferences, ChatGPT can offer customized recommendations, encourage additional sales, or provide exclusive offers.

Extending its utility to personalized marketing initiatives, ChatGPT aids in formulating bespoke emails or messages that resonate with individual customer narratives and historical engagement. Whether it's suggesting products or crafting unique promotions, ChatGPT's linguistic generation prowess enables you to dispatch compelling, targeted communication on a mass scale.

By tapping into ChatGPT for lead nurturing and automating customer-centric interactions, sales and marketing teams can unlock the platform's potential to refine workflows, amplify lead quality, and deliver unparalleled customer service.

Revolutionizing Customer Engagement with AI in Sales and Marketing

In the contemporary marketplace, where the speed and precision of customer service can set a brand apart, advancements in Artificial Intelligence (AI) have emerged as a game-changer for customer support dynamics. This segment delves into the transformative impact of two AI-driven solutions—ChatGPT and AI-enhanced chatbots—on customer support frameworks.

1. Deploying ChatGPT for Prompt, Accurate Customer Interactions

ChatGPT, a sophisticated language model, harnesses machine learning to mimic and generate responses that are indistinguishably human. Training ChatGPT on a comprehensive compendium of customer inquiries and associ
ated data primes it to handle common questions with speed and accuracy.

When customers initiate contact, ChatGPT rapidly interprets their questions, delivering instant solutions drawn from its extensive training. This diminishes wait times and promotes customer self-service. Integrating ChatGPT for routine queries allows customer support personnel to allocate more time to intricate issues, offering tailored support where it's most needed.

2. AI-Enhanced Chatbots for Efficient Support Ticket Resolution

Support ticket management can be daunting, particularly when faced with a deluge of simultaneous requests. AI-enhanced chatbots are invaluable in such scenarios, adept at addressing straightforward and repetitive customer questions, thus freeing up human agents to concentrate on complex, higher-stakes tasks.

These chatbots, powered by Natural Language Processing (NLP), intelligently comprehend and process customer tickets. They can guide users through troubleshooting procedures or elevate the issue to a human colleague if the situation demands. The initial automation of interactions by these chatbots slashes response times and boosts overall operational efficiency.

Additionally, these AI-driven chatbots are designed to evolve through continuous interaction, accumulating data to refine and perfect their responses. This progressive learning ensures an ever-improving capacity for issue resolution, leading to increased customer satisfaction.
By integrating AI solutions like ChatGPT and AI-powered chatbots into customer support strategies, businesses can fundamentally transform client interactions. Offering swift, precise responses and streamlined ticket management not only elevates the customer experience but also enhances service efficiency, driving stronger customer loyalty and satisfaction.

Optimizing Project Management with AI Technologies

Project management is an intricate dance of coordinating tasks, facilitating clear communication, and fostering teamwork. The emergence of Artificial Intelligence (AI) equips project leaders with innovative tools that bolster their ability to manage projects more effectively. We will examine how AI, particularly through ChatGPT for task organization, and AI-enhanced tools for collaboration, can be potent aids in the project management arena.

1. Streamlining Task Organization with ChatGPT

ChatGPT, an advanced language model trained on extensive datasets, offers project managers a sophisticated method to refine task delegation. With ChatGPT, the process of distributing tasks can be automated, matching the right tasks with suitable team members efficiently.

Understanding project scopes, assessing available resources, and recognizing individual skill sets are within ChatGPT's capabilities. It can recommend task assignments by evaluating team members' competencies and availability, allowing for strategic decision-making in task distribution, which amplifies team efficiency.

Beyond assignment, ChatGPT can serve as an oversight mechanism. Integrated with project management software, it can track progress, flag deadlines, and identify challenges, empowering managers to preemptively tackle issues and maintain project momentum.

2. Enhancing Team Collaboration with AI-Driven Tools

The heart of project success lies in seamless team collaboration. AI-driven collaboration tools significantly improve how team members interact and coordinate their efforts.

These tools support real-time communication and help synchronize team activities, ensuring collective focus and aligned objectives. By implementing AI in project management, leaders can enhance coordination, boost productivity, and optimize resource allocation. The results are expedited project timelines, cost reductions, and elevated client satisfaction.

By embracing ChatGPT for task management and AI tools for team synergy, project managers can refine their workflow, navigate challenges more effectively, and consistently lead projects to triumphant completions within allotted timeframes and budgets.

Other Industries and Job Functions

Advancing Decision-Making and Problem-Solving Across Sectors

ChatGPT can play a pivotal role in the decision-making process within various industries and job roles by delivering insights, deciphering complex datasets, and drawing upon historical patterns to inform choices. Here's how it can make a significant impact:

 1. *Generating Insights:* ChatGPT can digest and interpret vast quantities of data, extracting pivotal insights. For instance, when fed with sales figures, it can pinpoint trends, consumer behaviors, or areas ripe for enhancement. These insights can clarify the broader picture, informing and refining your decision-making trajectory.

 2. *Facilitating Data Analysis*: ChatGPT can aid in the distillation and arrangement of data, transforming it into actionable intelligence. It has the ability to navigate through intricate datasets, execute analytical computations, and spotlight correlations or tendencies that may be hidden. This capability is instrumental in revealing critical insights that can steer data-informed choices.

 3. *Learning from Historical Trends:* With its training on a variety of data, ChatGPT can recognize and understand historical trends and patterns. When faced with new decisions or challenges, it can consult these learned pattern

Optimizing Time and Task Management with ChatGPT

ChatGPT can be an invaluable asset for employees aiming to enhance their organizational skills, manage time wisely, and keep abreast of their duties. Let's explore the ways ChatGPT can contribute to better time and task management:

1. Improving Time Management: ChatGPT can offer employees strategies to manage their schedules more effectively by analyzing their workload and impending deadlines. For instance, if an employee is juggling multiple assignments, ChatGPT can devise a schedule or pinpoint which tasks demand immediate focus.

2. Assisting with Task Prioritization: Cha.tGPT can provide counsel on task prioritization. By reviewing an employee's to-do list, ChatGPT can help identify which tasks are most critical or urgent, considering various factors like impending deadlines, task interdependencies, and the potential impact of each task.

3. Enabling Reminders: ChatGPT can serve as an automated reminder system, ensuring employees remain aligned with their duties. It can set alerts for specific tasks or milestones, providing timely notifications to prevent oversight of essential responsibilities.

4. Streamlining Task Organization: ChatGPT can aid in structuring tasks by overseeing a to-do list or task management framework. Employees can add and track task status, and converse with ChatGPT about their progress. ChatGPT can also offer organizational strategies, such as categorizing tasks by project, urgency, or other pertinent criteria, aiding in prioritization and systematic organization.

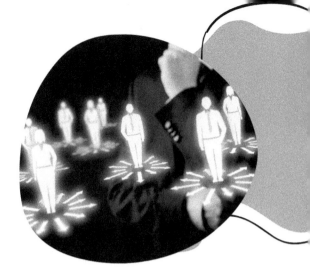

Enhancing Decision-Making with ChatGPT Assistance

ChatGPT can act as a sophisticated support system, providing valuable insights and recommendations to streamline decision-making across various domains such as resource distribution, strategic planning, and creative problem-solving. Here's how ChatGPT can be instrumental:

1. Optimizing Resource Allocation: ChatGPT can enhance the decision-making process regarding resource distribution by evaluating available assets, project demands, and potential limitations. With the appropriate input, ChatGPT can guide the efficient allocation of budgets, personnel, or materials, drawing from established patterns and sector-specific best practices to ensure that resources are utilized to their fullest potential for superior project results.

2. Streamlining Project Planning: In the realm of project management, ChatGPT can contribute by formulating task lists, setting timelines, and mapping dependencies. Engaging with the details of a project allows ChatGPT to construct comprehensive project outlines, spotlight possible hurdles, and provide solutions to circumvent risks, taking into account elements such as the duration of tasks, resource accessibility, and ultimate project objectives to craft realistic and impactful project strategies.

3. Facilitating Problem-Solving: When confronted with challenges, ChatGPT's capability to analyze and offer solutions becomes particularly advantageous. Describing the issue to ChatGPT allows it to apply pattern recognition, refer to historical successes, and propose viable resolutions. It can be a source of inspiration for ideation sessions or for considering alternate methods in complex problem scenarios.

4. Data-Driven Learning and Recommendations: With its extensive training in diverse data sets, ChatGPT is adept at extrapolating insights and applying them to novel situations, making it a powerful tool for informed decision-making. This capacity enables ChatGPT to present contextual advice and strategic options based on proven methodologies and successes in comparable circumstances.

Advancing Personal Development and Knowledge Acquisition with ChatGPT

ChatGPT stands as a catalyst for continuous personal growth, serving as a gateway to educational content, industry developments, and authoritative insights, thereby aiding employees in skill enhancement and staying at the forefront of their fields. Here's how ChatGPT can be a cornerstone for ongoing education:

1. Accessing Educational Resources: ChatGPT can provide a wealth of educational resources such as articles, instructional content, multimedia, and more. Employees can request information on particular subjects they wish to explore, and ChatGPT can deliver pertinent resources to broaden their understanding, facilitating autonomous learning and skill advancement.

2. Staying Informed on Sector Developments: ChatGPT can be a conduit for the latest sector-specific news and updates. Employees can engage in dialogue about certain subjects, prompting ChatGPT to supply current insights on new trends, market dynamics, regulatory revisions, or technological breakthroughs, keeping employees in sync with their industry's pulse.

3. Gleaning Expert Opinions: Having assimilated a broad spectrum of information, including specialist insights, ChatGPT can act as a portal to expert knowledge. Employees can consult ChatGPT for advice on particular challenges or for recommendations derived from expert viewpoints. Although it doesn't replace direct human mentorship, ChatGPT can offer an entry point to diverse perspectives and a breadth of expert knowledge.

4. Personalized Skill Enhancement Guidance: ChatGPT can advise on skill development tailored to an individual's interests, professional objectives, and present competencies. By discussing their career ambitions or identifying skill deficiencies, employees can receive personalized advice on the most pertinent skills to acquire or competencies to refine, thus customizing their learning trajectory.

Navigating the Complexities of AI Integration: Addressing ChatGPT's Challenges

Incorporating AI solutions like ChatGPT into the workplace involves navigating certain complexities to guarantee their beneficial and ethical application. Here are some pivotal challenges to consider:

1. Iterative Improvement and Precision Tuning: AI entities like ChatGPT necessitate ongoing refinement based on user interaction to bolster their utility and address shortcomings. Gathering user input systematically and updating the AI model can refine its responsiveness and pertinence. Periodic adjustments, informed by user feedback, can enhance ChatGPT's functionality, yielding more pertinent and dependable outcomes.

2. Bias Identification and Rectification: AI models, including ChatGPT, may unintentionally exhibit biases inherent in their training datasets. Vigilance against such biases is essential, with strategies to minimize their impact. Employing meticulous data selection, implementing bias detection methodologies, and consistent oversight can curtail biases and promote impartial and fair AI interactions. Routine evaluations are recommended to pinpoint and rectify any bias-related issues.

3. Ensuring Data Integrity and Confidentiality: The deployment of AI technologies necessitates the handling and storage of data, raising concerns about security and privacy. Strong security protocols must be established to guard sensitive information and comply with privacy standards. Measures such as access restrictions, data encryption, and strict adherence to data protection policies are pivotal in protecting sensitive information and upholding user confidentiality.

4. Maintaining Human Supervision and Responsibility: Though AI tools offer substantial capabilities, they are not intended to supplant human discernment and accountability. Human oversight is critical to scrutinize and corroborate AI-generated decisions or suggestions. Creating explicit accountability structures and educating the workforce on AI's limitations and correct usage can foster a responsible and informed AI deployment.

Optimal Strategies for Deploying ChatGPT in the Professional Sphere

Instituting ChatGPT within your organizational framework can significantly bolster productivity and streamline operations. To leverage this advanced tool effectively, adherence to strategic best practices is crucial. These guidelines will ensure precise, reliable engagement, safeguard user privacy, and ensure conformity with organizational norms. Here's a compendium of fundamental strategies to enhance the deployment of ChatGPT in your business environment.

1. Define Objectives Precisely: Ascertain the specific aims for deploying ChatGPT, such as bolstering customer service, generating content, or facilitating internal support. Targeted goals lead to more strategic deployment and refined interactions.

2. Tailor Training for ChatGPT: Enhance the base model with a wealth of quality, bespoke organizational data to fine-tune context comprehension and response accuracy. Continuously update the model with fresh data to escalate its efficacy.

3. Establish Usage Protocols: Formulate explicit protocols for ChatGPT's application to promote uniformity and adherence to organizational policies. Outline acceptable content parameters, interaction tone, and known limitations, disseminating these protocols among all stakeholders.

4. Implement Supervision Measures: Vigilantly monitor ChatGPT-user dialogues to certify the delivery of precise and suitable responses. Introduce a moderation framework to detect and address any potential discrepancies or biases in AI-generated content.

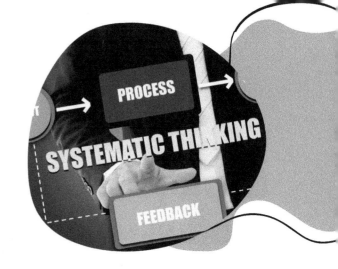

5. Promote Feedback Loops: Invite and value employee feedback regarding the relevance and quality of ChatGPT's outputs. This reflective process is pivotal for ongoing enhancement and iterative updates of the model.

6. Caution Against Overdependence: Recognize ChatGPT's utility while advising against its sole reliance. Encourage critical evaluation and corroboration of information to circumvent inaccuracies.

7. Uphold Privacy Standards: Ensure stringent security practices to protect user privacy. Be vigilant that sensitive data isn't improperly disclosed in interactions with ChatGPT or retained unnecessarily.

8. Independently Validate Information: Despite ChatGPT's capacity for providing useful insights, independent verification of crucial data or advice is essential. Corroborate with trustworthy sources and apply critical assessment to affirm the veracity and dependability of ChatGPT's responses.

9. Prepare Contingency Measures: Anticipate scenarios where ChatGPT may not deliver the requisite knowledge or insight. Maintain ready access to alternative resources to guarantee uninterrupted assistance to users in such instances.

10. Assess Performance Systematically: Routinely appraise ChatGPT's performance against key metrics like response precision, user satisfaction, and operational efficiency. Utilize this analysis to refine training protocols and enhance ChatGPT's application in your professional milieu.

Explore 100 Creative Uses for ChatGPT Right Now

1. Answer Frequently Asked Questions:
Prompt: Can you explain the return/exchange policy using the following summary? [Insert a summary of your company's policy]

2. Draft and Refine Communications:
Prompt: Can you provide suggestions for improving the flow of my executive summary? [Insert your executive summary]

3. Create Meeting Outlines and Decks:
Prompt: Could you help me create a slide deck outline for our upcoming sales team meeting? [Insert details about the meeting objectives and attendees]

4. Generate Team-Building Ideas:
Prompt: Can you suggest some creative team-building activities that our department can participate in? [Provide some information about your department's size and interests]

5. Provide Deadline Reminders:
Prompt: Could you remind me about the deadline for submitting the project proposal? [Specify the project name and the date the proposal is due]

6. Conduct Industry Research:
Prompt: Can you gather information on the latest trends in digital marketing? [Specify the specific aspect or subtopic in digital marketing you're interested in]

7. Plan Company Events:
Prompt: Could you help me with planning our annual holiday party? [Include any preferences or requirements for the party, such as date, time, location, and expected number of attendees]

8. Ideate Blog and Social Media Content:
Prompt: Can you provide some blog post ideas related to customer experience? [Specify any specific focus areas or target audience for the blog content]

9. Assist with Data Organization:

Prompt: Can you help me organize the customer data spreadsheet? [Specify the specific criteria or format for organizing the data]

10.Provide Training Resources:

Prompt: Can you provide a step-by-step guide on how to create a new deal in our CRM? [Specify the CRM platform being used and any specific requirements or fields to consider]

11. Suggest Employee Recognition Programs:

Prompt: What are some creative ways we can recognize and appreciate our employees' hard work and achievements? [Provide some background information on the company culture and the number of employees]

12. Assist with Meeting Scheduling:

Prompt: Can you help me find a time that works for everyone to schedule a team meeting? [Specify the desired meeting duration, the participants' availability, and any preferred dates or times]

13. Recommend Team Productivity Tools:

Prompt: Can you suggest some tools or software that can help our team collaborate and stay organized? [Specify any specific features or requirements]

14. Assist with Customer Support Inquiries:

Prompt: Can you help me respond to a customer's support ticket about a billing issue? [Provide necessary details like the customer's name and the specific issue]

15. Generate Internal Communication Improvements:

Prompt: What are some creative ways we can enhance communication among different departments in our company? [Provide any current challenges or pain points in communication]

16. Create Project Timelines:

Prompt: Can you assist me in creating a timeline for our upcoming marketing campaign? [Specify the campaign start and end dates, key milestones, and any dependencies]

17. Optimize Email Marketing Campaigns:
Prompt: Can you give me some tips on improving our email open rates and click-through rates? [Specify any specific challenges or current performance metrics]

18. Assist with Lead Generation Strategies:
Prompt: Can you suggest some effective lead generation tactics for our sales team? [Provide any target audience or industry information]

19. Recommend Professional Development Resources:
Prompt: Can you suggest some online courses or training programs for improving leadership skills? [Specify any specific focus areas or desired outcomes]

20. Organize Digital Files and Documents:
Prompt: Can you assist me in organizing our shared drive and creating a standardized naming convention? [Specify any existing categories or folder structure]

21. Assist with Marketing Material Creation:
Prompt: Can you help me write engaging copy for our upcoming product brochure? [Provide any specific details or key features that should be highlighted]

22. Ideate Remote Team Bonding Activities:
Prompt: Can you suggest some virtual team-building activities for our remote employees? [Provide information on the number of remote employees and any tools or platforms available for virtual activities]

23. Recommend Project Management Software:
Prompt: What project management software would you recommend for our team to improve productivity and collaboration? [Specify any specific features or integrations needed]

24. Assist with Market Research:
Prompt: Can you help me gather information on our top competitors and their marketing strategies? [Specify the industry or market segment and any key competitors]

25. Ideate Employee Wellness Programs:

Prompt: Can you suggest some initiatives or activities to promote employee wellness and work-life balance? [Provide information on the company's current wellness programs or initiatives]

26. Create Customer Satisfaction Surveys:

Prompt: Can you assist me in designing a customer satisfaction survey to gather feedback on our products and services? [Specify any specific questions or metrics to include]

27. Recommend Customer Retention Strategies:

Prompt: What are some effective strategies or tactics to improve customer retention for our business? [Provide any information on current customer churn rates or challenges]

28. Assist with Social Media Scheduling:

Prompt: Can you help me schedule our social media posts for the upcoming week? [Specify the social media platforms and any specific content or hashtags to include]

29. Optimize Website Conversion Rates:

Prompt: Can you give me some suggestions on how to increase our website's conversion rates? [Provide any specific pages or areas of the website to focus on]

30. Recommend Collaboration Tools for Remote Teams:

Prompt: What tools or platforms would you recommend for our remote team to collaborate effectively? [Specify any specific features or integrations needed]

31. Manage Email Campaigns:

Prompt: Can you help me design and send out our monthly newsletter to our subscribers? [Provide any specific content or promotions to be included]

32. Ideate Large Company Retreat Activities:

Prompt: Can you suggest some engaging activities for our company retreat with over 200 employees? [Provide any specific location or theme for the retreat]

33. Streamline Internal Processes:

Prompt: What are some ways we can simplify and streamline our project approval process? [Provide any current pain points or bottlenecks in the process]

34. Manage Online Advertising Campaigns:
Prompt: Can you help me set up and optimize our Google Ads campaign? [Specify any specific campaign goals or target audience]

35. Improve Customer Onboarding:
Prompt: Can you give me some suggestions on how to enhance our customer onboarding experience? [Provide any current challenges or pain points in onboarding]

36. Recommend Team Training Programs:
Prompt: Can you suggest some training programs or workshops to enhance our team's skills and knowledge? [Provide any specific areas or skills to focus on]

37. Assist with Data Analysis and Reporting:
Prompt: Can you help me analyze and summarize our monthly sales data? [Specify any specific metrics or reports required]

38. Generate Cross-Selling or Upselling Strategies:
Prompt: Can you give me some recommendations on how to effectively cross-sell or upsell our products? [Provide any information on current customer purchasing patterns]

39. Recommend Employee Engagement Initiatives:
Prompt: What are some initiatives or programs we can implement to improve employee engagement and morale? [Provide any current challenges or feedback from employee surveys]

40. Conduct Market Segmentation Analysis:
Prompt: Can you help me identify and define our target audience for a new product launch? [Specify any specific demographics or psychographics to consider]

41. Recommend Time Management Techniques:
Prompt: What are some effective time management techniques or strategies that can help improve productivity and efficiency? [Specify any specific challenges or areas where time management is needed]

42. Optimize Landing Pages for Lead Capture:
Prompt: Can you help me create a high-converting landing page for our upcoming lead generation campaign? [Provide any specific content or design preferences]

43. Ideate Employee Recognition and Rewards:
Prompt: Can you suggest some creative ways to recognize and reward our employees for their hard work and achievements? [Provide information on the company's budget and any existing recognition programs]

44. Improve Customer Service and Support:
Prompt: What are some best practices or strategies to enhance our customer service and support efforts? [Provide any specific feedback or areas of improvement]

45. Manage a Content Calendar for Social Media:
Prompt: Can you help me create a content calendar for our social media platforms for the next quarter? [Specify the desired posting frequency and any key events or promotions]

46. Improve Employee Feedback Processes:
Prompt: Can you give me some suggestions on how to make our employee feedback and performance review process more effective and meaningful? [Provide any specific challenges or feedback from employees]

47. Conduct A/B Testing and Optimization:
Prompt: What are some best practices for conducting A/B testing and optimizing our website or marketing campaigns? [Provide any specific elements or metrics to focus on]

48. Manage Customer Segmentation:
Prompt: Can you help me segment our customer database based on specific criteria for our upcoming targeted marketing campaign? [Specify the desired segmentation criteria or target audience]

49. Boost Remote Employee Engagement:
Prompt: Can you give me some suggestions on how to boost employee engagement and motivation in a remote work setup? [Provide any specific challenges or feedback from employees]

50.Improve Email Deliverability Rates:
Prompt: What strategies or best practices can improve our email deliverability rates and avoid being marked as spam? [Provide any specific challenges or email marketing platforms being used]

51. Create Customer Loyalty Programs:

Prompt: How can we design and implement a customer loyalty program to reward our repeat customers? [Provide any specific rewards or incentives to consider

52. Enhance Website Usability:

Prompt: What ways can you suggest to enhance the usability and user experience of our website? [Specify any specific pain points or user feedback]

53. Remote Team Communication Tools:

Prompt: Which communication and collaboration tools would you recommend for our remote team to stay connected and productive? [Specify any specific features or integrations needed]

54. Manage Customer Feedback Surveys:

Prompt: How can we design a customer feedback survey to gather insights on our products and services? [Specify any specific questions or metrics to include]

55. Improve Sales Conversion Rates:

Prompt: What suggestions can you provide to increase our sales conversion rates and close more deals? [Provide any specific sales processes or metrics to focus on]

56. Improve Website SEO:

Prompt: What strategies or tactics can improve our website's SEO and increase organic traffic? [Provide any specific keywords or competitors to consider]

57. Develop Customer Referral Programs:

Prompt: How can we develop a customer referral program to incentivize our existing customers to refer new leads? [Provide any specific rewards or incentives to offer]

58. Enhance Employee Onboarding:

Prompt: What suggestions can you offer to enhance our employee onboarding experience and make it more efficient? [Provide any specific challenges or pain points in onboarding]

59. CRM Strategies:

Prompt: What are the best practices or strategies for managing and nurturing customer relationships using our CRM system? [Specify the CRM platform being used and any specific challenges or goals]

60. Create Customer Advocacy Programs:
Prompt: How can we develop a customer advocacy program to empower and mobilize our loyal customers to promote our brand? [Provide any specific rewards or incentives to offer and any existing customer base]

61. Employee Training and Development:
Prompt: What suggestions do you have for enhancing our employee training and development programs to foster continuous learning and growth? [Provide any specific areas or skills to focus on and any existing training initiatives]

62. Optimize Website Performance:
Prompt: What strategies or tools can we use to improve our website's loading speed and overall performance? [Specify any specific challenges or metrics to focus on]

63. Customer Retention Campaigns:
Prompt: How can we design and execute a customer retention campaign to reduce churn and increase loyalty? [Provide any specific offers or messages to include]

64. Team Recognition Activities:
Prompt: What creative ways can you suggest to recognize and appreciate our team members' contributions and accomplishments? [Provide any specific team size or dynamics]

65. Remote Team Collaboration Tools:
Prompt: Which collaboration and project management tools would you recommend for our remote team to streamline workflows and stay organized? [Specify any specific features or integrations needed]

66.Influencer Marketing Campaigns:
Prompt: How can we identify and collaborate with relevant influencers for our marketing campaigns? [Specify the target audience and any specific goals or budge

67. Customer Experience and Satisfaction:
Prompt: What suggestions do you have for enhancing our overall customer experience and ensuring satisfaction? [Provide any specific pain points or feedback from customers]

77. Streamlining Business Workflows:

Prompt: What tools or technologies can we use to automate and streamline our business workflows and processes? [Provide any specific pain points or inefficiencies in current workflows]

78. Email Marketing Automation Workflows:

Prompt: How can we set up and optimize our email marketing automation workflows to improve engagement and conversions? [Specify any specific segmentation or triggers to consider]

79. Customer Retention Enhancement:

Prompt: What suggestions do you have for enhancing our customer retention and loyalty programs to increase customer lifetime value? [Provide any specific challenges or current program details]

80. Website Accessibility Improvements:

Prompt: What strategies or techniques can make our website more accessible for users with disabilities? [Specify any specific accessibility guidelines or regulations to follow]

81. Customer Satisfaction Surveys:

Prompt: How can we design and implement a customer satisfaction survey to gather feedback on our products or services? [Provide any specific questions or rating scales to include]

82. Collaboration and Teamwork:

Prompt: What suggestions do you have for fostering better collaboration and teamwork among our employees? [Provide any specific challenges or team dynamics]

83. Customer Touchpoints Optimization:

Prompt: What strategies or tactics can optimize our customer journey and ensure positive touchpoints along the way? [Provide any specific touchpoints or stages of the customer journey]

84. Customer Rewards Programs:

Prompt: How can we develop a customer loyalty and rewards program to incentivize repeat purchases and customer retention? [Provide any specific rewards or incentives to offer]

85. Work-Life Balance Improvements:

Prompt: What suggestions do you have for promoting employee wellness and work-life balance in our organization? [Provide any specific challenges or feedback from employees

86. Email Marketing Automation and Personalization:

Prompt: What are the key practices or techniques for enhancing our email marketing automation and personalization efforts? [Specify any specific personalization variables or segmentation criteria]

87. Complaint Resolution Process Management:

Prompt: How can we design an effective customer feedback and complaint resolution process to address concerns and improve satisfaction? [Provide any specific channels or escalation procedures]

88. Website Conversion Funnel Optimization:

Prompt: What suggestions do you have for optimizing our website conversion funnels and increasing conversion rates? [Provide any specific funnel stages or metrics to focus on]

89. Customer Service Response Time Optimization:

Prompt: What strategies or tools can we use to improve our customer service response times and ensure timely resolutions? [Provide any specific challenges or average response time metrics]

90. Internal Communication Improvement:

Prompt: How can we enhance communication between different teams or departments? [Provide some information about the challenges or areas for improvement]

91. Productivity Apps and Tools:

Prompt: What project management tools can help streamline our workflow? [Specify any specific requirements or integration preferences]

92. Email Management and Organization:

Prompt: What tips can you provide for keeping my inbox organized and managing email overload? [Specify any specific challenges you're facing or desired email management practices]

93. Efficient Meeting Agendas:

Prompt: How can we create a well-structured meeting agenda for our weekly team meeting? [Include any specific discussion topics or goals for the meeting]

94. Time Management Techniques:

Prompt: What tips can you recommend for effectively managing time during busy periods? [Specify the specific challenges or time constraints you're facing]

95. Troubleshooting Technical Issues:

Prompt: How can we troubleshoot an issue with connecting to our CRM system? [Include any error messages or specific information about the problem]

96. Templates for Documents and Presentations:

Prompt: How can we create a template for our weekly sales report presentation? [Specify any specific formatting or content requirements]

97. Project Delegation Best Practices:

Prompt: What are the best practices for delegating tasks to team members without micromanaging? [Include any specific concerns or challenges you're facing]

98. Prioritizing Customer Feedback:

Prompt: How can we effectively gather and categorize customer feedback? [Specify any specific channels for feedback collection or desired categorization criteria]

99. Tracking Key Performance Indicators:

Prompt: How can we set up a dashboard to track and visualize our sales team's performance metrics? [Specify the specific KPIs you want to track and any desired visualization formats]

100. Enhance Digital Security Measures:

Prompt: What steps can we take to improve our digital security and protect sensitive company data? [Provide any specific areas of concern or current security measures in place]

Follow-up Prompts

There are 1100 prompts that you can use as follow-ups in order to get more specific or revised information from ChatGPT and other Chatbots. Don't forget to tailor these prompts to your specific circumstances and to the response you previously received from the Chatbot.

Each of these prompt types serves a different purpose and can be used effectively in different scenarios. Depending on the context and the intended outcome, one type of prompt may be more suitable than another.

These prompts are divided into eleven distinct categories, each tailored to specific conversational needs: Generic, Enhancement, Clarification, Probing, Critical Thinking, Instructional, Exploration, Comparison, Summarization, Evaluation, and Hypothetical.

To have access to 1100 follow-up prompts, please scan this QR code:

SHARE YOUR INSIGHTS

Invest a minute to enhance someone's productivity journey. Your insights can guide professionals in navigating complex work environments and seeking effective productivity strategies.

If "Elevate Your Productivity Using ChatGPT" has helped streamline your tasks or innovate your workflow, please share your experiences in a review. Your feedback can:

- Direct others to effective productivity tools and techniques.
- Help individuals master AI-driven efficiency.
- Transform professional lives through enhanced task management.

Enjoyed the book? Scan the QR code to leave a review where you purchased it. Your review is invaluable and helps foster a community of productivity-focused professionals.

Thank you for contributing to a more efficient and productive world.

Best regards,

Mauricio

www.ingramcontent.com/pod-product-compliance
Lightning Source LLC
LaVergne TN
LVHW060125070326
832902LV00019B/3139